Thomas Aquinas:
Philosopher, Theologian, Saint

Thomas Aquinas, also known as Saint Thomas Aquinas, was a prominent medieval philosopher and theologian whose profound impact on Western thought continues to resonate to this day. He was born in the year 1225 or 1226 in the Castle of Roccasecca, located in the Kingdom of Sicily (present-day Italy), into a noble family. His parents, Landulf and Theodora, provided him with a rich upbringing, instilling in him a sense of discipline and devotion to the Christian faith.

At the age of five, Thomas was sent to the Benedictine monastery of Monte Cassino to receive his early education. During his time there, he exhibited exceptional intellect and a keen interest in learning. However, his education at Monte Cassino was interrupted by political unrest in the region, which led to the monastery being besieged.

After his time at Monte Cassino, Thomas continued his education at the University of Naples, one of the most prestigious academic institutions of the time, where he studied a variety of subjects including arithmetic, music, and astronomy. It was here that he was exposed to the works of Aristotle, the Greek philosopher whose ideas would profoundly influence Thomas's intellectual development. Thomas's encounter with Aristotelian philosophy sparked a lifelong engagement with reason and logic, which he would later synthesize with Christian theology in his own philosophical writings.

In 1244, Thomas made a momentous decision to join the Dominican Order, a choice that greatly disappointed his family, who had hoped he would pursue a lucrative secular career. Despite their objections, which even led to his brief arrest in the family castle, Thomas remained resolute in his commitment to a life of religious devotion and scholarly pursuit. He continued his studies within the Dominican Order, first at Naples and later at the University of Paris, where he had the opportunity to study under the renowned philosopher Albertus Magnus.

During his time in Paris, Thomas distinguished himself as a brilliant scholar and prolific writer. He delved deeply into both theology and philosophy, seeking to reconcile faith with reason and to elucidate the relationship between God and the natural world. His intellectual prowess and theological insights earned him widespread acclaim within academic circles, establishing him as one of the leading thinkers of his time.

As Thomas's reputation grew, so too did his influence. He became known for his ability to navigate complex theological and philosophical issues with clarity and precision, earning him the title "the Angelic Doctor." Throughout his life, Thomas remained dedicated to the pursuit of truth, viewing philosophy and theology not as separate disciplines but as complementary avenues to understanding the divine mysteries.

Scholarly Contributions and Legacy

Thomas Aquinas's magnum opus, the Summa Theologica, stands as a monumental achievement in the history of theology and philosophy. Comprising over one and a half million words, this comprehensive work systematically addresses nearly every aspect of Christian doctrine and morality. Written in the form of a series of questions and answers, the Summa reflects Thomas's rigorous analytical approach and his commitment to clarity and precision.

One of the key themes of the Summa Theologica is the reconciliation of faith and reason. Thomas argued that faith and reason are not contradictory but complementary, with each serving as a guide to truth in its own right. Drawing heavily on the works of Aristotle, Thomas developed a philosophical framework that sought to harmonize the teachings of the Church with the insights of classical philosophy.

Another of Thomas's central achievements was his development of the philosophy of natural law, which posits that certain moral principles are inherent in human nature and can be known through reason. Drawing on Aristotle's ethical theory, Thomas argued that humans possess a natural inclination toward the good and that moral principles can be discerned through rational reflection on the nature of humanity and the world. This idea would profoundly influence later moral philosophers and theologians, shaping debates on ethics and political theory for centuries.

In addition to his contributions to moral philosophy, Thomas Aquinas made significant advances in metaphysics, epistemology, and philosophy of religion. His rigorous use of reason and logical argumentation to explore theological mysteries earned him acclaim as one of the greatest philosophical minds of the Middle Ages. Thomas's philosophical writings continue to be studied and debated by scholars of philosophy and theology, inspiring new avenues of inquiry and interpretation.

In the centuries following his death in 1274, Thomas Aquinas was canonized as a saint by the Catholic Church, and his feast day is celebrated on January 28th. He is also honored as a Doctor of the Church, a title reserved for those whose teachings have made a significant impact on Christian theology.

Throughout the centuries, Thomas Aquinas's thought has continued to inspire individuals from diverse backgrounds and disciplines. His commitment to the pursuit of truth, his rigorous application of reason to matters of faith, and his profound insights into the nature of God and humanity ensure that his legacy endures as a beacon of intellectual and spiritual enlightenment for generations to come. Thomas Aquinas remains not only a towering figure in the history of philosophy and theology but also a guiding light for all who seek wisdom and understanding in the pursuit of truth.

Major Ideas and Philosophy of Thomas Aquinas

SCHOLASTICISM: Scholasticism, a prominent intellectual movement in the Middle Ages, aimed to reconcile faith with reason and integrate Christian theology with classical philosophy, particularly that of Aristotle. Thomas Aquinas emerged as a leading figure in the Scholastic tradition, emphasizing the use of reason and argumentation to explore theological and philosophical questions. In his writings, such as the Summa Theologica, Aquinas engaged in systematic inquiry, organizing theological topics into logical frameworks and presenting arguments supported by philosophical principles. Scholastic philosophers like Aquinas sought to demonstrate the compatibility of faith and reason, showing that theological truths could be illuminated and enriched by philosophical inquiry. By synthesizing Christian theology with Aristotelian philosophy, Aquinas contributed to the development of Scholastic thought and influenced subsequent generations of philosophers and theologians.

NATURAL THEOLOGY: Natural theology, central to Aquinas's philosophy, asserts that reason, guided by philosophy, can lead to knowledge of God and his attributes. Aquinas believed that humans could attain knowledge of God's existence through observation and rational reflection on the natural world. He famously formulated Five Ways, or Five Proofs, as arguments for the existence of God, drawing on principles of causality, contingency, and order in the universe. For instance, in the First Way, Aquinas argues from the observed motion in the world to the existence of an unmoved mover, which he identifies as God. Through natural

theology, Aquinas sought to demonstrate the rational basis for belief in God, showing that religious truths could be supported by philosophical reasoning grounded in the natural order.

METAPHYSICS: Aquinas's metaphysics, deeply influenced by Aristotle's philosophy, explores fundamental questions about the nature of being, substance, essence, existence, and causality. He developed a comprehensive metaphysical system that seeks to understand the ultimate principles underlying reality. Central to Aquinas's metaphysics is the distinction between essence and existence, a key concept inherited from Aristotle. Aquinas argues that while creatures have distinct essences (what they are) and existences (that they exist), in God, essence and existence are identical. Furthermore, Aquinas introduces the concept of act and potency, which he uses to explain change and causality in the world. According to Aquinas, everything in the world is composed of actuality (act) and potentiality (potency), and change occurs when potentiality is actualized. Through his metaphysical inquiries, Aquinas seeks to provide a systematic account of reality, grounded in reason and informed by philosophical principles, reflecting his commitment to understanding the nature of existence and the ultimate causes of things.

EPISTEMOLOGY: Epistemology is the branch of philosophy concerned with the nature, origin, and scope of knowledge. Thomas Aquinas addressed epistemological questions about how humans acquire knowledge and the limitations of human understanding. He posited that humans could attain

knowledge of the natural world through sensory experience and empirical investigation.

For Aquinas, sensory experience provides the foundation for empirical knowledge, allowing individuals to perceive and understand the physical world through their senses. Additionally, Aquinas emphasized the role of reason and intellect in acquiring knowledge of metaphysical truths. He believed that human beings possess rational faculties that enable them to engage in intellectual abstraction and reasoning, leading to insights into abstract concepts and universal truths. Through reason and intellect, Aquinas argued, individuals could come to understand fundamental metaphysical principles, such as the existence of God and the nature of the soul.

ETHICS: Aquinas's ethical theory is grounded in natural law, a moral theory that posits an objective standard of morality rooted in human nature and discernible through reason. He believed that moral principles are inherent in the rational order of the universe, reflecting the divine plan for human conduct. According to Aquinas, human beings have a natural inclination to pursue the good and avoid evil, which is manifested in their rational capacity to discern moral truths. Central to Aquinas's ethical framework are the cardinal virtues and theological virtues. The cardinal virtues—prudence, justice, fortitude, and temperance—are moral virtues that govern human actions and guide individuals toward virtuous behavior. Aquinas argued that these virtues are cultivated through reason and enable individuals to lead morally upright lives. In addition to the cardinal virtues, Aquinas identified the theological virtues—faith, hope, and charity—as infused virtues that are bestowed upon individuals by divine grace. These virtues enable individuals to transcend their natural capacities and orient their lives toward God, fostering spiritual growth and moral excellence.

PHILOSOPHY OF MIND AND SOUL: Aquinas's philosophy of mind and soul delves into fundamental questions about the nature of human consciousness, the immaterial aspect of human beings, and the relationship between the mind (soul) and the body. Central to Aquinas's understanding is the concept of the human soul as the immaterial, rational principle that animates the body and gives it life. In Aquinas's dualistic view of human nature, the soul is distinct from the body and is characterized by its rational faculties, including intellect and will. Unlike the physical body, which is subject to change and decay, the soul is immortal and persists beyond the death of the body. Aquinas argued for the immortality of the soul based on its incorporeal nature and its capacity for intellectual activity, which he believed transcends the limitations of the material world. Aquinas also explored the relationship between the soul and the body, rejecting both a strict dualism that posits the complete separation of the soul and body, and a strict materialism that denies the existence of the soul altogether. Instead, he proposed a holistic view in which the soul and body are united in a substantial union, with the soul serving as the form of the body, giving it its particular identity and animating its activities.

DIVINE SIMPLICITY: Divine simplicity is a fundamental doctrine in Aquinas's theology that affirms the absolute unity and simplicity of God's nature. According to Aquinas, God is pure actuality, devoid of any potentiality or composition. This means that God is not composed of parts, attributes, or qualities, but rather is identical with his attributes and essence. In affirming divine simplicity, Aquinas rejects any notion of multiplicity or complexity within God's being. Instead, he argues that God is infinitely perfect and lacks any kind of composition or division. All of God's attributes—such as his goodness, wisdom, and omnipotence—are identical with his essence, and there is no distinction between them. This doctrine has profound implications for Aquinas's understanding of God's nature and attributes. It underscores God's transcendence and absolute perfection, affirming that God is not subject to change or limitation and is the ultimate source of all reality.

JUST PRICE: The concept of the "just price" was a significant aspect of Thomas Aquinas's economic thought, rooted in his ethical framework and understanding of justice. Aquinas believed that economic transactions should be guided by principles of fairness, equity, and the common good, rather than merely by market forces or individual self-interest. According to Aquinas, the just price of a good or service should reflect its true value, taking into account factors such as the cost of production, the quality of the goods, and the needs of both buyers and sellers. He rejected the idea that prices should be determined solely by supply and demand, arguing instead that prices should be regulated by moral considerations and the principles of distributive justice. Aquinas's concept of the just price was closely linked to his broader ethical theory, which emphasized the importance of virtue and moral integrity in economic affairs. He believed that economic transactions should be conducted with honesty, integrity, and concern for the well-being of others, reflecting his commitment to the principles of natural law and the common good.

DETERMINATIO: Determinatio, within Thomistic philosophy, encapsulates the process of applying general moral principles to specific situations, thus translating abstract ethical ideals into practical guidance for moral decision-making. This concept underscores Thomas Aquinas's emphasis on prudence, wherein moral judgments are not merely deduced from universal principles but rather discerned through careful consideration of particular circumstances. For instance, consider the ethical dilemma of truth-telling in a sensitive situation. While honesty is a foundational moral principle, determinatio requires assessing factors such as the potential harm caused by divulging certain information and the individual's duty to protect others from harm. Through determinatio, one navigates the complexities of moral choices, striving to uphold ethical principles while considering the nuances of each unique circumstance. In this way, determinatio reflects Aquinas's holistic approach to moral reasoning, integrating abstract principles with practical wisdom to guide virtuous action.

THOMISTIC SACRAMENTAL THEOLOGY: Thomistic sacramental theology refers to Thomas Aquinas's theological framework for understanding the sacraments within the Catholic Church. Sacraments are regarded as sacred rituals instituted by Christ to confer grace upon believers, and Aquinas's theology seeks to elucidate their significance, efficacy, and theological underpinnings. Central to Aquinas's sacramental theology is the concept of sacramental causality, which holds that sacraments are efficacious signs that communicate the grace they signify. Aquinas distinguished between the instrumental cause of the sacraments (the physical elements and actions involved) and the principal cause (Christ himself, who confers grace through the sacraments). Aquinas identified seven sacraments—Baptism, Confirmation, Eucharist, Penance, Anointing of the Sick, Holy Orders, and Matrimony—and elucidated their theological significance and effects. He emphasized the sacraments as visible signs of God's grace, efficacious channels of divine life and healing, and means of sanctification for the faithful.

In this book, we have compiled the essential quotes of Thomas Aquinas for your convenient reading, aiming to help you understand the philosophy and ideas of Aquinas more comprehensively. These quotes have been carefully curated to provide insight into Aquinas's thoughts, allowing readers to delve deeper into his profound theological and philosophical contributions.

The study of truth requires a considerable effort - which is why few are willing to undertake it out of love of knowledge - despite the fact that God has implanted a natural appetite for such knowledge in the minds of men.

God's precepts are light to the loving, heavy to the fearful.

Perfection of moral virtue does not wholly take away the passions, but regulates them.

To bear with patience wrongs done to oneself is a mark of perfection, but to bear with patience wrongs done to someone else is a mark of imperfection and even of actual sin.

Arrive at knowledge over small streamlets, and do not plunge immediately into the ocean, since progress must go from the easier to the more difficult.

The highest manifestation of life consists in this: that a being governs its own actions. A being that is always subject to the direction of another is somewhat of a dead thing.

Love works in a circle, for the beloved moves the lover by stamping a likeness, and the lover then goes out to hold the beloved in reality. Who first was the beginning now becomes the end of motion.

Peace is the work of justice indirectly, in so far as justice removes the obstacles to peace; but it is the work of charity (love) directly, since charity, according to its very notion, causes peace.

Pray thee, spare, thyself at times: for it becomes a wise man sometimes to relax the high pressure of his attention to work.

The theologian considers sin mainly as an offence against God; the moral philosopher as contrary to reasonableness.

If a thing can be done adequately by means of one, it is superfluous to do it by means of several; for we observe that nature does not employ two instruments if one suffices.

Art is simply a right method of doing things. The test of the artist does not lie in the will with which he goes to work, but in the excellence of the work he produces.

Virtue is not concerned with the amount of pleasure experienced by the external sense, as this depends on the disposition of the body; what matters is how much the interior appetite is affected by that pleasure.

Charity stands as the embodiment of love's highest calling, yet not all expressions of love attain the sanctified virtue of charity.

A man does not always choose what his guardian angel intends.

All the efforts of the human mind cannot exhaust the essence of a single fly.

It is evident
that if a man practice
a pitiful affection
for animals, he is all
the more disposed to
take pity on his
fellow-men.

It would be superfluous to receive by faith, things that can be known by natural reason.

The things we hold dear are mirrors of our essence, and reveal who we truly are.

Well ordered self-love, whereby man desires a fitting good for himself, is right and natural; but it is inordinate self-love, leading to contempt of God, that is the cause of sin.

There is a more perfect intellectual life in the angels. In them the intellect does not proceed to self-knowledge from anything exterior, but knows itself through itself....

Man cannot live without joy. That is why one deprived of spiritual joys goes over to carnal pleasures.

It is not possible to be ignorant of the end of things
if we know their beginning.

First, I say that he draws near to those who make peace with him. For God is the One who brings about peace; and where else should peace dwell than in peace?

Fear is such a powerful emotion for humans that when we allow it to take us over, it drives compassion right out of our hearts.

God is not related to creatures as though belonging to a different "genus," but as transcending every "genus," and as the principle of all "genera."

We should love others truly, for their own sakes rather than our own.

Every truth without exception -- and whoever may utter it -- is from the Holy Spirit.

An angel can illuminate the thought and mind of man by strengthening the power of vision, and by bringing within his reach some truth which the angel himself contemplates.

An act of love always tends towards two things; to the good that one wills, and to the person for whom one wills it.

It is requisite for the relaxation of the mind that we make use, from time to time, of playful words or deeds.

Happiness is secured through virtue; it is a good attained by man's own will.

God has no need for our worship. It is we who need to show our gratitude for what we have received.

Where senses falter,
in shadows'
silent reign,
Faith's gentle
whisper reveals
His presence,
eternal
and untamed.

Doubts about faith often arise not from the uncertainty of truths but from our limited understanding, akin to an owl dazzled by sunlight. Nevertheless, even a glimpse of profound matters outweighs the surest knowledge of lesser ones.

How is it they live in such harmony the billions of stars — when most men can barely go a minute without declaring war in their minds about someone they know.

See to whom Jesus is drawing near, three kinds of people: to those who make peace with him, to those who are devoted to God, and to those who are kind to their neighbors.

Within the depths
of every soul,
an unrelenting
longing persists,
seeking both the
sweet nectar of joy
and the profound
depths of purpose.

God ought not to be labeled as an individual entity, since the principal of individuation is matter.

All that I have written seems like straw compared to what has now been revealed to me.

Believing is an act of the intellect assenting to the divine truth by command of the will moved by God through grace.

In the fabric of existence, one essence prevails,
Self-necessitated, no external chains entail.
It shapes all existence, from the stars to the sod,
In reverence, humanity names it simply: God.

Justice is a certain rectitude of mind whereby a man does what he ought to do in the circumstances confronting him.

One aspect of
neighbourly love
is that we must not
merely will our
neighbours good,
but actually work
to bring it about.

Errors arise from two main sources: either the foundation of an argument is flawed, rooted in misinformation or falsehood, or the argument itself is poorly constructed, lacking coherence or logical development.

Man has free choice,
or otherwise counsels,
exhortations,
commands,
prohibitions,
rewards and
punishments
would be in vain.

In the lover's gaze, the beloved finds refuge, while the lover, entranced, becomes one with the beloved, seeking to unveil the mysteries within their soul.

Man is closer to God according to his existence in grace than he is according to his existence in nature.

Pain itself can be pleasurable accidentally in so far as it is accompanied by wonder, as in stage-plays; or in so far as it recalls a beloved object to one's memory, and makes one feel one's love for the thing, whose absence gives us pain. Consequently, since love is pleasant, both pain and whatever else results from love, in so far as they remind us of our love, are pleasant.

When the devil is called the god of this world, it is not because he made it, but because we serve him with our worldliness.

The law of nature is nothing other than the light of the intellect planted in us by God, by which we know what should be done and what should be avoided. God gave us this light or law in creation.

Being born he gave himself as our Companion, Eating with us he gave himself as Food, Dying He became our Ransom, Reigning he gives himself as our Reward.

Love is a binding force, by which another is joined to me and cherished by myself.

Eternity is called whole, not because it has parts, but because it is lacking in nothing.

But virtue's true reward is happiness itself, for which the virtuous work: whereas if they worked for honor, it would no longer be a virtue, but ambition.

It is a sin directly against one's neighbour, since one man cannot over-abound in external riches, without another man lacking them.

We must love them both, those whose opinions we share and those whose opinions we reject, for both have labored in the search for truth, and both have helped us in finding it.

A thing is lovable according as it is good. But God is infinite good. Therefore He is infinitely lovable.

The greatest kindness one can render to any man consists in leading him from error to truth.

All my words are but chaff next to the faith of a simple man.

Just as it is better to illuminate than merely to shine, so to pass on what one has contemplated is better than merely to contemplate.

It would seem that zeal is not an effect of love. For zeal is a beginning of contention.

How can we live in harmony? First we need to know we are all madly in love with the same God.

It is not theft, properly speaking, to take secretly and use another's property in a case of extreme need: because that which he takes for the support of his life becomes his own property by reason of that need.

To stray from conscience's guiding light is to tread the path of sin.

Grace does not destroy nature but perfects it.

He who is not angry when there is just cause for anger is immoral. Why? Because anger looks to the good of justice. And if you can live amid injustice without anger, you are immoral as well as unjust.

I would rather feel
compassion than know
the meaning of it.
I would hope to act
with compassion
without thinking
of personal gain.

Fear of God is
not the beginning
of wisdom.

The Study of
philosophy is not
that we may know what
men have thought, but
what the truth of
things is.

The surplus bread you withhold is the rightful provision of the hungry; the clothing you conceal is the due attire of the naked; and the money you hoard in the earth is the means of redemption and succor for the destitute.

If all evil were prevented, much good would be absent from the universe. A lion would cease to live, if there were no slaying of animals; and there would be no patience of martyrs if there were no tyrannical persecution.

In the depths of ignorance, desire ignites, A fire within, as the soul takes flight. Through self-discovery's sacred embrace, The joy of learning, in each step, we trace.

Miracles are signs not to them that believe, but to them that believe not.

No man truly has joy unless he lives in love.

In the grand theater of existence, the soul takes its stage,
Its essence laid bare, not by words, but deeds engage.
Through every gesture, every choice made whole,
The soul's true essence, by its acts, it does unfold.

Every man is not bound to imperil his own body for his neighbor's safety: this belongs to the perfect.

If the highest aim of a captain were to preserve his ship, he would keep it in port forever.

Beauty adds to goodness a relation to the cognitive faculty: so that "good" means that which simply pleases the appetite; while the "beautiful" is something pleasant to apprehend.

The highest perfection of human life consists in the mind of man being detached from care, for the sake of God.

For in order that man may do well, whether in the works of the active life, or in those of the contemplative life, he needs the fellowship of friends.

Even as in the blessed in heaven there will be most perfect charity, so in the damned there will be the most perfect hate. Wherefore as the saints will rejoice in all goods, so will the damned grieve for all goods. Consequently the sight of the happiness of the saints will give them very great pain.

Music is the
exaltation of the
mind derived from
things eternal,
bursting forth
in sound.

The greatness of the
human being consists
in this: that it is
capable of the
universe.

Sloth is sluggishness of the mind which neglects to begin good...it is evil in its effect, if it so oppresses man as to draw him away entirely from good deeds.

Because we cannot know what God is, but only what He is not, we cannot consider how He is but only how He is not.

Because philosophy arises from awe, a philosopher is bound in his way to be a lover of myths and poetic fables. Poets and philosophers are alike in being big with wonder.

Distinctions drawn by the mind are not necessarily equivalent to distinctions in reality.

God destines us for an end beyond the grasp of reason.

Friendship is
the source of the
greatest pleasures,
and without friends
even the most
agreeable pursuits
become tedious.

Charity, by which God and neighbor are loved, is the most perfect friendship.

Moral science is better occupied when treating of friendship than of justice.

Knowledge is according to the mode of the one who knows; for the thing known is in the knower according to the mode of the knower.

True fulfillment in life arises from finding joy and satisfaction in the labor we undertake.

Love takes up where knowledge leaves off.

The meaning of what is said is according to the motive for saying it: because things are not subject to speech, but speech to things.

Grant me, O Lord my God, a mind to know you, a heart to seek you, wisdom to find you, conduct pleasing to you, faithful perseverance in waiting for you, and a hope of finally embracing you. Amen.

Further, nothing, except sin, is contrary to an act of virtue. But war is contrary to peace. Therefore war is always a sin.

Those suited for an active life can cultivate contemplation through their actions, while those inclined to contemplation can engage in active endeavors to deepen their spiritual understanding.

To love is to
will the good
of the other.

To disparage the
dictate of reason
is equivalent to
contemning the
command of God.

Wonder was the motive that led people to philosophy ... wonder is a kind of desire in knowledge. It is the cause of delight because it carries with it the hope of discovery.

Due to the boundless nature of divine goodness, it could not be fully depicted by a single creature. Thus, God created a multitude of diverse beings, each contributing to the portrayal of divine goodness in its own unique way. While goodness is singular and unified in God, it manifests diversely among creatures. Therefore, the collective universe more completely embodies and reflects the divine goodness than any individual entity alone.

The knowledge of God is the cause of things. For the knowledge of God is to all creatures what the knowledge of the artificer is to things made by his art.

We ought to cherish the body. Our body's substance is not from an evil principle, as the Manicheans imagine, but from God. And therefore, we ought to cherish the body by the friendship of love, by which we love God.

Law: an ordinance of reason for the common good, made by him who has care of the community.

Charity is the form, mover, mother and root of all the virtues.

Additional Reading

A look at major works by Thomas Aquinas to encourage further exploration by the reader.

SUMMA THEOLOGICA (Summa Theologiae): Thomas Aquinas's Summa Theologica stands as one of the most monumental and enduring works in Western philosophy and theology. Spanning over 1.5 million words, this comprehensive synthesis of Christian theology and philosophy is divided into three main parts: the First Part, the Second Part (which is further divided into two sections), and the Third Part. Each part is meticulously organized into questions, which are then subdivided into articles, facilitating a systematic exploration of theological and philosophical topics. In the Summa Theologica, Aquinas embarks on a profound inquiry into fundamental theological doctrines and principles, covering a vast array of topics that include the existence and nature of God, the mysteries of creation, the complexities of human nature, the principles of ethics and morality, the functioning of law and governance, the workings of divine grace, the significance of sacraments, and the contemplation of eschatological themes.

Central to Aquinas's approach in the Summa Theologica is his dialectical method, characterized by the presentation of questions, objections, and responses. Each article is meticulously structured around a series of arguments and counterarguments, reflecting Aquinas's commitment to thorough examination and logical rigor. By engaging with various viewpoints and anticipating potential objections, Aquinas demonstrates his mastery of theological argumentation and his ability to navigate complex theological and philosophical terrain. The Summa Theologica is celebrated for its clarity, precision, and systematic approach to theological inquiry. Aquinas's writing style is marked by lucid exposition and meticulous argumentation, making his profound insights accessible to readers across generations. Moreover, the Summa Theologica serves as a foundational text in Catholic theology, providing a comprehensive framework for theological study and reflection.

Aquinas's synthesis of faith and reason is a hallmark of the Summa Theologica, as he draws upon both Christian revelation and Aristotelian philosophy to elucidate theological truths. His integration of philosophical wisdom with theological insight exemplifies his commitment to the harmony between faith and reason, a principle that continues to shape theological discourse and philosophical inquiry in the modern era.

SUMMA CONTRA GENTILES (Summa Against the Gentiles): Written as a defense of the Christian faith against non-Christian beliefs, particularly Islam and Judaism, the Summa Contra Gentiles showcases Aquinas's prowess as a theologian and philosopher engaged in interreligious dialogue. Unlike the Summa Theologica, which is primarily intended for Christian scholars and students, the Summa Contra Gentiles is aimed at a broader audience, including skeptics, unbelievers, and adherents of other religions. In this work, Aquinas systematically presents arguments for the truths of the Christian faith, drawing upon both reason and revelation. He engages with the philosophical and theological perspectives of non-Christian traditions, offering critiques and rebuttals while seeking common ground where possible. The Summa Contra Gentiles demonstrates Aquinas's dedication to intellectual rigor, rational argumentation, and the pursuit of truth across religious boundaries.

COMMENTARIES ON ARISTOTLE: Thomas Aquinas's commentaries on Aristotle's works are significant for their role in reintroducing Aristotelian philosophy to the West and for Aquinas's innovative synthesis of Aristotelian thought with Christian theology. Aquinas produced commentaries on several of Aristotle's works, including Metaphysics, Physics, Nicomachean Ethics, and De Anima, among others. In these commentaries, Aquinas elucidates Aristotle's philosophical ideas, offering interpretations, clarifications, and critical reflections. He seeks to reconcile Aristotelian principles with Christian doctrine, demonstrating the compatibility of faith and reason. Aquinas's commentaries are characterized by their systematic exposition, logical analysis, and theological insights, reflecting his commitment to integrating philosophical wisdom with theological truth. Aquinas's commentaries on Aristotle played a crucial role in the revival of Aristotelianism in the West, influencing subsequent generations of scholars and shaping the development of Western philosophy and theology. His synthesis of Aristotelian philosophy with Christian theology remains a cornerstone of Scholastic thought and a testament to Aquinas's intellectual legacy.

DE ENTE ET ESSENTIA (On Being and Essence): In "De Ente et Essentia", Thomas Aquinas undertakes a concise yet profound exploration of fundamental metaphysical questions concerning the nature of being and existence. Drawing heavily from the philosophical framework of Aristotle, Aquinas seeks to elucidate the distinction between "being" (esse) and "essence" (essentia) and to examine their interrelationship. In this work, Aquinas analyzes the ontological status of entities, probing the essence of things and their existence. He explores the concept of essence as the defining characteristic or nature of a thing, and existence as the act of being or actuality that brings a thing into existence. Through careful analysis and logical argumentation, Aquinas seeks to elucidate the metaphysical principles underlying reality and the nature of existence itself. "De Ente et Essentia" is characterized by its rigorous philosophical inquiry and its synthesis of Aristotelian metaphysics with Christian theology. It exemplifies Aquinas's resolve to employing reason and rational analysis in the exploration of theological and philosophical questions, laying the groundwork for his broader metaphysical system articulated in works such as the "Summa Theologica."

SUMMA THEOLOGIAE AD FRATRES PRAEDICATORES (Compendium of Theology for the Friars Preachers): "Summa Theologiae ad Fratres Praedicatores" represents a condensed version of Aquinas's monumental "Summa Theologica." Intended for the practical use of his fellow Dominicans, particularly the Friars Preachers, this work provides a more accessible overview of Aquinas's theological insights and teachings. In this

compendium, Aquinas presents a systematic exposition of key theological doctrines and principles, covering topics such as the nature and attributes of God, creation, human nature, morality, grace, and sacraments. Unlike the extensive and detailed format of the "Summa Theologica," the "Summa Theologiae ad Fratres Praedicatores" offers a concise and condensed treatment of theological topics, making it suitable for teaching and study within the Dominican Order. Despite its brevity, this compendium retains the clarity, logical structure, and systematic approach characteristic of Aquinas's larger works. It serves as a valuable resource for theologians, scholars, and students seeking a comprehensive overview of Aquinas's theological thought, particularly within the context of Dominican theological education and practice.

DISPUTED QUESTIONS: Aquinas wrote several sets of disputed questions on various theological and philosophical topics, which showcase his dialectical skill and his ability to engage with complex issues through rigorous debate and analysis. These works consist of questions posed by Aquinas or his students, followed by objections and responses, demonstrating Aquinas's method of argumentation and his willingness to engage with diverse perspectives. The disputed questions cover a wide range of theological and philosophical topics, including God's existence, the nature of the soul, divine providence, predestination, grace, and sacraments, among others. Aquinas approaches each question with precision and clarity, drawing upon both reason and revelation to provide nuanced and insightful answers. Through his engagement with disputed questions and their structured format, Aquinas seeks to clarify theological and philosophical issues, promote critical thinking, and deepen understanding within the broader intellectual community of his time.

DE POTENTIA (ON POWER): In "De Potentia", Aquinas undertakes a thorough examination of the nature of divine power and its relationship to human free will. This treatise offers profound insights into theological concepts such as omnipotence, providence, and the relationship between God's will and human actions. Aquinas explores the nature of divine power as it relates to God's attributes, particularly omnipotence—the divine ability to accomplish all things. He grapples with questions concerning the compatibility of divine omnipotence with human freedom and the problem of evil. Aquinas also discusses the concept of divine providence, examining how God's power interacts with the course of human history and the unfolding of events in the world. "De Potentia" reflects Aquinas's deep engagement with theological and philosophical questions surrounding the nature of God and the relationship between the divine and the created order. Through careful analysis and logical argumentation, Aquinas seeks to elucidate the mysteries of divine power and its implications for human existence.

SCRIPTUM SUPER LIBROS SENTENTIARUM (Commentary on the Sentences of Peter Lombard): Aquinas's "Scriptum Super Libros Sententiarum" is a comprehensive commentary on Peter Lombard's "Sentences," a standard theological textbook of the time. In this commentary, Aquinas provides insights into his early theological development and his engagement with theological debates of the period. Aquinas's commentary on the "Sentences" demonstrates his mastery of theological scholarship and his ability to engage critically with the ideas of his predecessors. He offers detailed exegesis and analysis of Lombard's text, providing clarifications, rebuttals, and theological insights. The commentary also serves as a platform for Aquinas to articulate his own theological views and to develop his distinctive theological synthesis. "Scriptum Super Libros Sententiarum" is a foundational work in Aquinas's corpus, reflecting his early theological formation and his emerging theological methodology.

It provides valuable insights into Aquinas's intellectual development and his contributions to medieval theology, laying the groundwork for his later masterpieces such as the "Summa Theologica."

DE REGNO AD REGEM CYPRI (On Kingship to the King of Cyprus): In "De Regno ad Regem Cypri", Thomas Aquinas offers a comprehensive treatise on the nature and purpose of kingship, addressing political theory and governance from a Christian perspective. This work is dedicated to the King of Cyprus, offering guidance on the principles of just rule and the responsibilities of secular authority. Aquinas argues for the legitimacy of secular authority, affirming the role of kingship as ordained by God for the common good of society. He emphasizes the importance of moral virtue and the rule of law in ensuring the stability and righteousness of governance. Aquinas explores the relationship between the king and his subjects, advocating for a balanced exercise of authority guided by principles of justice, prudence, and

benevolence. "De Regno ad Regem Cypri" reflects Aquinas's dedication to integrating theological principles with political philosophy, providing insights into his understanding of the proper role of secular authority in relation to divine law and natural law. It remains a significant work in medieval political thought, addressing timeless questions about the nature of political authority and the obligations of rulership.

Left incomplete due to the death of Aquinas, "De Regno ad Regem Cypri" touches on the right to revolt if a ruler were to act against the common good of the people, reflecting Aquinas's nuanced understanding of political governance and the conditions under which resistance to authority may be justified in pursuit of justice and the common good. Though unfinished, the insights offered in this work contribute to Aquinas's broader exploration of the principles of just governance and the ethical responsibilities of rulership.

DE VIRTUTIBUS (On Virtues): "De Virtutibus" is a significant work by Thomas Aquinas that explores the nature of virtues and their role in the moral life. Drawing on his synthesis of Aristotelian ethics and Christian theology, Aquinas provides a comprehensive account of virtue ethics, outlining the cardinal virtues and theological virtues and examining their significance for moral character and conduct. In this treatise, Aquinas distinguishes between different types of virtues, including moral virtues (such as prudence, justice, fortitude, and temperance) and theological virtues (faith, hope, and charity), and discusses their acquisition and cultivation through habituation and divine grace. He explores the relationship between virtue and happiness, arguing that virtuous living leads to true fulfillment and flourishing. "De Virtutibus" exemplifies Aquinas's resolve to integrating philosophical wisdom with theological insight, providing a robust framework for ethical reflection and moral formation. It remains a foundational work in virtue ethics, offering valuable insights into the nature of moral virtue and its importance for the spiritual and ethical life.

EXPOSITIO SUPER JOB AD LITTERAM (Commentary on the Book of Job): Aquinas's "Expositio super Job ad litteram" is a profound commentary on the biblical Book of Job, offering theological reflections on the themes of suffering, divine providence, and the problem of evil. The Book of Job is renowned for its exploration of the nature of human suffering and the divine response to the existence of evil in the world, making it a fitting subject for Aquinas's philosophical and theological inquiry. In this commentary, Aquinas provides a detailed analysis of the text of Job, examining its narrative structure, poetic language, and theological implications. He grapples with the existential questions raised by Job's plight, including the nature of suffering, the justice of God, and the mystery of divine providence. Aquinas seeks to elucidate the theological significance of Job's experiences and to offer insights into the human condition in light of divine revelation. Central to Aquinas's commentary is his exploration of the problem of evil, addressing questions about the existence of evil in a world created by a benevolent and omnipotent God. He draws upon philosophical and theological resources to provide a nuanced understanding of the relationship between human suffering and divine providence, emphasizing the role of faith and trust in God's plan.

Printed in Great Britain
by Amazon